Mother,
One More Thing

Mother, One More Thing

Poems by Carla Schwartz

Turning Point Books

Published by Turning Point Books
P.O. Box 541106
Cincinnati, OH 45254-1106

ISBN: 9781625490728
LCCN: 2014932035

Poetry Editor: Kevin Walzer
Business Editor: Lori Jareo

Front Cover Photography: Carla Schwartz
Front Cover Design Concept: Carla Schwartz
Front Cover Graphic Design Finishing: Blake Reeves
Back Cover Photography: Claude von Roesgen

Visit us on the web at www.turningpointbooks.com
Author's website: www.carlapoet.com

About the Author

Carla Schwartz is a poet, poetry filmmaker, photographer, and lyricist. Originally from New York, she has made the Boston area her home. Her film work incorporates poetry and video. Her YouTube channel videos have had thousands of views. Carla is a professional writer with a doctoral degree in electrical engineering from Princeton. She is also an avid outdoors enthusiast, swimmer, cyclist, chef, and gardener. You can find out more from her website at carlapoet.com.

Dedication

This book is dedicated to the memory of my mother, Helga Schwartz: beauty, artist, mathematician, feminist, activist. I will always have one more thing to tell you.

Thanks

There are so many to thank. My teachers: Peter Campion, Martha Collins, Cornelius Eady, Fred Marchant, Carl Phillips, Nick Flynn, Mark Doty, Dorianne Laux, Maxine Kumin, Gail Mazur, and especially Alan Feldman, in whose workshop I drafted many of these poems. Thank you, too, to all of the workshop participants I have shared poems with. Also thanks to my friends in poetry, Aimée Sands, Jim Henle, Kathrine Douthit, John Anderson, Susana Roberts, Ann and Joe Killough, Frannie Lindsay, Michael Mack, Kim and Frank Garcia, Tam Neville, Burt Stern, Alyson Adler, Tom Daley, and Nicole Terez Dutton. Special thanks to the special eyes of early readers, Lea Banks, Jenny Mackenzie, Frannie Lindsay, Susana Roberts, Michael Mack, and Tam Neville. Thank you Mel and Heidi for your love and support. I could not have done this without you. Thank you all the Winklers for being such fine gatherers. Thanks to Blake Reeves for your fine graphic design work. Thank you folks at WordTech Communications. And finally, thanks to Claude, for revealing my inner princess.

Acknowledgments

The author is grateful for the publication of earlier versions of the following poems:

"Counting," *Stone Highway Review*, issue 1.3, June 2012, p. 58.
"Décolletage," *Equinox*, Fall 2008 edition, p. 180.
"Figs in June," *Stone Highway Review*, issue 2.3, June 2013,
    p. 46.
"Ginger Beer," *Literary Juice*, October, 2012.
"Green Dress," *Fulcrum 7*, p. 189.
"In the Café," *Common Ground Review*, Fall/Winter, 2013.
"Lily Finds a Story About Jack on the Internet," *Cactus Heart*,
to appear.
"Mother, He Spins Me Around," "Knockoff," "Night Swim,"
    and "Fall Leaves," *Boston Poetry Magazine*,
http://bostonpoetry.wordpress.com/tag/carla-schwartz/,
    October 14, 2013, and forthcoming in the *Boston Poetry
    Magazine Anthology*.
"Not to Complain," *Emerge Literary Review*, issue four,
October 2012, p. 30.
"The Flirt," *Stone Highway Review*, issue 2.2, January 2013,
    p. 52.
"Tina," *Enizagam*, 2011, p. 141.

Table of Contents

I. History of Raspberries

II. The Hard Side of Yellow

III. Décolletage

IV. What Mother Didn't Know

I. History of Raspberries

Raspberry Satisfaction

And if they start their cycle of blooms and pollen
from budding green leaf to bunches of stubbly beards
and prickly vines in June, would I reap a bounty
of the pure red, the candy red, and the tight pinks
on tongue, on finger, splattered on shirt all summer – or

would the leaf rust tamp my dreams of sweet berry-
brained July and August, the dearth overshadow the
anticipation of abundant harvest, and only one or two
berries appear, while bees pay homage daily
to the fruitless plants, thirsty in summer's heat,

until I remember there are two crops, one autumnal,
herculean, compared to Summer's paltry one, when the
berries come daily, like the mail, first in triples, and by
October, small pails full to pluck and suck and melt
between palette and tongue, the need for teeth,
obviated, and the bees, tired from months-long travails,
asleep on the leaves all day, not a flower left,
just bouquets of tight green rasp-fists waiting to ripen,
my red treasures nabbed before berry meets kitchen,
except when missed under leaf, one clings, hidden?

In the Café

If I don't read K's email
while working in a café today,
then soft wind on my face.

If the note isn't prefaced
by her declination of my invitation,
then alternator current.

The fireplace calls *liar* when I pass by,
the unlit sculpture slumped in its char.

Show us your heart
   a beach stone.
Show us your smile
   a coiled ribbon.

Love is a blouse of dismissed calls,
it flatters. What island are we from
that with just two of us
we don't see each other?

A nanosecond is only as big
as a pencil. If the mouth
has no brain behind it,
   then blueberries.

We have no reason
to leave, so we stay.
If K's father isn't in hospital,
   monarch butterfly.

The fire sculpture is stacked, waiting for K.
And if tears, then mother–
K proposes *bitter,* and I say *not bitter.*
A bear trading a paper flower for a newspaper:
>   *raw honey*
>   *clover honey*
>   *orange blossom*

If not my mother, then
wipe tears from the face of a woman
typing in a cafe.
If I call   then *dead woodchuck.*
>   *Show me the tissues.*
Show me
>   the tissues.

Withstanding the Heat

We all know how to put a dinner together.
At your house, it's simple,
not having much choice of ingredients.
I choose the fine pasta over rice,
a no-brainer, really, in terms of time.
I gather the box of pasta, comfortable on its shelf,
angel hair, even faster, and bring it to counter.
This time, I use the big pot, not the 2-quart,
to add wiggle room for what needs to wiggle now,
and later.

I set the full pot on the back burner to boil,
while I work the sauce. Your spice cabinet, full, but dull,
offers rice vinegar, soy sauce, and sesame oil,
the large skillet for the sauce and frozen vegetables.
The garlic in the refrigerator is turning. A brown film.
I point out the sepia edges. You defend the slime.
Not used to garlic in stiff plastic, I stab
the rusted steel knife into the package, and it resists.

The knife cuts through the plastic to my thumb,
and enters my skin.
My shriek startles you into unwilling action.
Accidents don't happen
in your house. The blood roses
bloom into the compress.
Your rescue: an insufficient band aid
and a child's lesson in cutting.
Red splashes on sour garlic.
When I return to the kitchen,
you have turned off the stove,
as if to imply I would burn the dinner.
It was only water wanting to boil,
a big pot of it, and that takes time.

Into the pan with the pressed garlic,
I add the almond butter, which clings to the spoon,
and the soy, the sesame oil, and vinegar.
I need something
in the hot pepper department. More red taint
for the almond sauce. I slit the bag of vegetables,
timidly now, and add them in. Stir. Heat.
I strain the pasta back into its pot.
When I toss in the vegetables,
you can't see the red.

A History of Raspberries

Frances lived in a little house
between Route 9 and the Pike.
She had been there 40 years,
through two kids, grown and gone.
Husband, dead. Cigarette habit, dead.
But her plantings thrived.

She was thinning raspberries one year,
and offered me some.
I made a place for these
to compete with my wild blacks
that I could take or leave.

When I lived in Vermont, I planted raspberries
in front of the bathtub Mary.
I don't know what the nuns next door
thought about that, but those berries were good.

It took three years before the first berries arrived
one October, just barely before the first frost.

In November, I put two soft plump ones
in a silver cardboard ring box
to bring to my mother, sick in hospital.

Her eyes lit on them as if they were holiday ornaments,
or truffles, or cherrystones on the half-shell.

Now, Frances is dead of lung cancer. Mom, leukemia.
I get a summer and fall crop of raspberries.
I had berries into December this year.

I still have the red-stained cardboard box.
Each bite, a sweet tart burst.
Frances. My mother. Bathtub Mary.

Figs in June

I used to say the only good reason to live in Florida
was fresh figs in June. I never told that to Frank.

Frank had a back yard pear tree.
The pears were spotted and misshapen.
He didn't eat them, so I could have all
I wanted. The tree was taller than his house,
so I had to take the drops. That was O.K.
Those pears would be good for a pie.

There were also two fig trees at the side of his yard
close to mine. Fig trees are short
with mushroom crowns.
The figs are hard and green and bitter until they ripen,
when they turn soft and sweet.

Frank didn't need no truck with the figs either.
But the birds, they was another story.
You might think the tree of knowledge was a fig.
Somehow the fig trees taught me outsmarting the birds.
They only gave for about one week in June.
I'd head out with my little green pint basket
and pick a day short of ripe.

Frank said, *One time I climbed up on my roof with my b.b.*
and shot a squirrel right off the tree.
I used to want the pears when my girls were young,
but the squirrels would eat 'em all first.

Addressing What's Broken

I wish
I were good
with tools,
so that when the stove
timer
doesn't keep time
anymore,
I would know
how to pull
off the knob
and recoil
the spring,
or set it straight
just so,
so that when I turn
the knob,
I can depend
on the ticking
of minutes,
the quiet panting
until the annoying mechanical buzz
saws
against the silence.

I wish
too, I could find
my refrigerator
model number,
and know how
to replace the door
gasket when it arrives.

For now
I am good
with duct tape.
It holds
two doors
kissing
when magnets
no longer attract.

Passports

After Sandra Kogut's film, "My Hungarian Passport"

1. Language

Unlawful to mutilate
is printed in English.

My mother's motherland was German,
now Polish,
and her girl eyes saw home fade away,
out the back of a taxi,
   to a train
   to a boat
   to island
with big cockroaches
landed here,
leathered in her daddy's suitcase.

Language was guarded
for secrets with her mom
and otherwise lost.

I learned twelve words of German
from Gramma, too:
Eine, nein, bluse, baum.

And here is a tree.
Plant firmly in ground.
And here I am,
a soiled American,
asking *Which country is my country?*

2. The Application

Forms available for download
in black and white,
German/English.

By what reason do you apply for citizenship?
Do they not trust the populace its own words?
How can I answer in multiple choice?
>   Mother's birth certificate
>   Grandmother's passport
>   Marriage certificate
Father? Brooklyn.
Mother? Gleiwitz.

Beautiful documents,
green pages, yellowed,
unfakeably stamped.

Each page tells a story:
A German mother with two young children.
Exit, Cuba.
Point of entry, Miami.

My mother's motherland
by virtue of its theft,
I hereby decree
Article two:
The laws of revocation.

I mail the application from a U.S. post office,
the day towers topple to rubble,
the day strangers outside of New York City don't touch.

3. The Passport Photo

The drugstore clerk snaps two poses:
    Teeth
    No teeth
He, whose ancestors wore teeth around their necks.
Me, trying to look stiff,
the fountain of brows,
the startled eyes,
the thin-lipped smile.
How German can I look?

4. The Day

The guard opens his border to me:
A six-by-eight room,
bullet-proof glass.
An office in a shopping center,
downtown Boston.
My point of entry,
if only I answer the questions correctly.
I am here to become a citizen
of your country.

In German I don't understand,
I smile,
I sign,
I apply for the passport,
and celebrate,
on my new country
(the Deputy Consul likes to eat)
Legal Seafood.

5. Reisepass

Reisepass,
now, Europäische:
Green pages
a printed weave
a chain threads,
waves.
On each page
the griffin/falcon,
fists raised,
head turned.
No question
who is citizen.
A union of order,
and difference.

6. European Passport

The book I garner,
given graciously.
Two years unused,
license
ticket
bears my likeness,
unstamped
untraveled
unquestioned.
The key to homeland,
not yet turned,
not dared to open,
to invite
Who are you to enter my country?

Midlife Harvest

Beans hang like tapers. Some bulge
their abacus beads. Count seven.
Some still slender, modest,
inconspicuous in their green youth.

The tangled vines droop. Twisted hunchbacks
in a huddle. Leaf veins purple, chlorophyll
leaching from their sticky hearts.

I step into the barely tended.
Hay grasses seed at the knees.
A Christmas of radish pods.
A few cherry tomatoes,
hard and green, clasp woody stalks.
Basil and peppers are shaded by the beans
I bend to gather singly or in pairs.

I tug at the vine, sometimes tear,
and drop them one by one,
mounting in my sack, and exit,
a bean leaf stamped on my chest.

.

Last Season's Gourd

Gray and white storm-washed colors,
long-necked mama, she all behind.

Wild turkey, pheasant, heron.
No head, she is attached to limb

by wire noose. A ghost
in window from this angle,

and up close, the dead
tangled umbilical lacks root.

Not lassoed, but carried
in one hand, by ladder.

Skin so hard, her seeds might die
before they ever touch soil.

Bittersweet

The vine twists and winds through the air,
its branches halved from previous cuts.
The spotted bark, papery skin,
sheaves of brown layered on tan.
So light this rope, flimsy swing,
what harm could it bring a pine?
What threat does this web portend?

From inattention,
the braided vines thicken.
How many times do you say, *Mother,*
I don't want to see you again, ever
before Mother expires?

The bittersweet strangles
under the umbrage of branches
and I don't notice.
The struggling pine succumbs,
limb by limb.

The vine at root is three inches thick.
I attack with a saw and count 23 rings.
The weed is itself a tree. Red-orange berries
triumph atop sixty feet of almost bare bark.

From Nectar

First the tenuous finger, long, slender,
green all summer.
Each leaf, a lacy sea, the pocked ravagings
daily by Japanese beetles, surely would yield no berry.

Late August, the upper curtains brittle.
The first plump sweets appear.
Paint fingers 40s lipstick red, stain tips candy.
Every few days, a few more jewels.

This raspberry bush, the sole yielding arm,
steady, dependable, mine.
Love undeclared, arms exposed, not yet victim
to the prickers' poison glyphs. Gingerly, I pick.

By October, three lower arms bloom and berry.
No frost harm yet, and I don't worry.
The season wanes.
I expect velvet caresses, daily.

In Defense of Peaches

My mother tied her socks
to the peach tree in front of her house.
I'm guessing she took sweaty ones
off her feet one day, or specially donned old ones,
and hung them, and an old shirt
to scare away squirrels and rabbits,
maybe after reading about it somewhere—
better than fox urine for sure.

The socks still hang on the tree.
Larvae lollipops.
None of us has thought to press
nose to cloth and inhale.
That was her last wish, to go outside.
Let whatever of mom still imbues, remain
and hang there year 'round, like her clay bells.

The other day, under my peach tree,
there were four hard ones, shaken down
and chewed as best a green stone can be.
Must have been a squirrel with a bad memory,
taking bite of one, and a next, leaving the unfinished
to ferment.

That same day, I discovered my shoe
was lucky. Twice lost in three months.
First on a mountain. Next, on a road.

Maybe I should nestle
those shoes into the crook of the peach
to fend off the wildlife.
Maybe my mother's climbing shoes will do.
Maybe this year I will be lucky
in peaches.

Elegy: Ann Before the Bends

Water that fills rivers and seas,
fill us with comfort,
flood out the town,
take it with eminent domain,
the barns, horses, pigs.
Be the desert lake we rowed lazily as children.

Fill where I earn my living,
be salty for buoyancy, weighty
in your dark depths where I lure
tourists suited in tanks, heavy in lead.

Fill my office with angel fish.
Sit down with an octopus.
Take me from the blessed raspberries I love.
Don't let me think about the food I will cook tonight.

Angel hair pasta, drizzled in olive oil
and mango chutney.
The bread I set out to rise
this morning needs a punch-down.
Take me far from all that. Steel my focus.

Water that fills my life with danger
        bend with me.
Fill me with hope.
Fill the earth with laughter.
Fill the space when I'm gone.

II. The Hard Side of Yellow

Daily Call

You would be calling me
out of the cold water today,
telling me to buy a new car,
as you did fifteen years ago,
before I bought the Honda.

I would be telling you
It only has 235 thousand,
and if I just replace the leaking fuel lines,
it will last to 300, at least.

You would parry with side airbags
and antilock brakes.
I still regret not having changed
the timing gear in the Chevelle.

Just then you would lament,
upset that my face is cut,
my eye, bruised, my legs, my palm,
and introduce me,
"This is my daughter, she fell off her bike."
The subtext reads, *She doesn't usually look like this,*
I'm embarrassed, forgive her.
Not buying into the healing powers of a cold pond,
you would insist I will get sick.

I can't call to say I won't let go of the Honda
because you helped me buy it
and you're not here anymore,
you, star of the showroom,
who knew how to say "no,"
to walk away from what you didn't want.

A Nap

The woman who lies down and closes her eyes
dreams of herself as a child napping.
Her breath, deep and heavy,
squirrel dust in small swirls under her nose.

The woman who thinks of her mother
on her mother's birthday
holds back tears that fall
against her will.

Dead mothers don't have to age.
Lucky them.
They spirit around without ever falling
and breaking a hip.

The woman thinks she is capable of a deep love.
She dreams she is a stone, rolling downhill.
She will drop up against the grass and wobble,
nuzzle the blades. A shying sun lashes her shadow.

Last Glass of Orange Juice

After she refused the hospital ice,
not believing it to be filtered,
after she spilled her fiction of my pregnancy
on all her friends,
after the hospital sent her home to die,
after she stopped eating almost altogether,
but before the hope of recovery eluded us in stealth,
I walked into her room with my morning juice,
which glowed for her as if lit from within,
and forgetting she was about to die,
she smiled up, and took a sip.

How We Learn

We mistake first, and then correct.
     Spelling
     Addition
     Stepping on toes
Avoiding an argument or making up.

When I first went to the cinema, three towns over,
I knew I could not be on time for a movie.

I took days of preparation
experienced the Zen of it
asking questions, studying maps.

The roads all twisted,
predicting the exit I didn't know
was westbound, but not east.

I missed it the first time.
The road map of my mind,
blank over there,
I lost myself
until at last I arrived
after the film had begun.

Now I can drive there from any direction. The roads,
as familiar as the plush seats, extend my right arm.

But how do we learn death, if it only happens once?
I can't say, *Next time, Ma, I will be there.* And Heidi.
And Dad. There won't be shouting and crying.

We will hold your hand as you pass in and out,
the air sucked away from you,
the walls of your blood, dissolved.

There will be seconds
when you don't throw your hand up
against the pain of touch.

Maybe you will hang on
just a minute longer
knowing we are there.

When I Swim in the Cold

When I swim in the cold, I swim in the cold,
I whim, and I zip, and I zim in the cold.
I flubber and glubber with every stroke.
I can feel my jelly-arms, but none of my toes.
I pull like a turtle, I kick like a duck.
I glide, skim, and slide over this icy blue flow.
I wonder this time, if I won't survive,
if this heart-stopping water will better me,
how dying where I find so much pleasure would be.
No time to think too much about this.
No time to let myself freeze.
I won't disappoint my plans to get old.
I pull with my will and swim in the cold.

Tina

Before I saw her red truck,
hood open, and the pink fur
slippers in the corner,

neatly anticipating feet, before
she told me she was waiting
for a call at three,

before I stole two hours
for a swim, I thought I'd be
alone on the porch.

Before the impossibility of solitude,
the instantly cluttered thoughts,
before the beating sun, and the inability to sit

still, after noticing the tofu,
new to the refrigerator shelf,
and the bags of fresh mushrooms and cauliflower,

after the introductions, the *you're staying here too?*s,
after Tina said she was there to feed the animals,
after *Excuse me*, after *My ex is a shit*

and is taking custody of my kids,
after the sound of the running tub,
I stopped counting on that view of the bay,

sheep, and cows, a quiet sit down with my pen.
After Tina attended her phone,
her story appeared in pieces

while I chopped bits of garlic on the counter.
Out of her idea of dinner, I led her to believe
I, too, would have put the mushrooms in last.

The Colander

1.

Sky polka dots through the star patterned holes
in the aluminum colander bowl,
bought a long time ago,
at Tags in Porter Square,
back in college
when we were steaming greens,
straining peas, playing house
until, wilted in the afternoon,
you, pretend husband, left.
I kept that sieve through all five moves,
the men, the chili, pasta al pesto, vichyssoise.

2.

I bought that Florida cracker house, in part,
for its property:
Lush palmetto jungle with wrap around creek.
One after-party mission, shark's teeth.

The closest tool at hand to sift the creek's mottled sand,
the old aluminum colander bowl.
We scattered, sifted,
and found ancient pieces of fossilized jaw bone.

Frank, next door, said our creek had been polluted,
Superfund. Frank, dead now, cancer.

The mustard brown creek scum,
crusted to the rough-hewn aluminum,
doesn't clean easy, try as I may,
spaghetti, next spaghetti, and the next.

Why didn't I pitch what I couldn't scrub clean?
Ten years later, the crud doesn't show anymore,
except maybe on internal x-ray.

I look at that colander
and see cancer,
Alzheimer's,
one or another of those men,
dancing with me in the kitchen.

November

The box descends
braced by planks
and strapped to hands,
square, thin, raw.
Pine, like all others like it,
except for the remains.

We commence the burial
with shovels full of sandy soil,
our final send-off to what now is just a corpse,
the body whose womb I traversed,
who held me through the worst turns.

I held her, those last days
when, to rays streaming through the room,
to Death itself,
my mother - joyous, rapt,
proposed the seeming impossible task:
Let's go outside!

The Lone Berry

The lone berry, he picked and sucked
like a cherry stone pit, then spit out,
was that her nipple he licked,
while on the phone with his mother,
lulled to a null sleep, until he rolled over
a burr in the grass, again, and again?

He re-rolled the burr,
none too soon, to find his finger
on her lone berry, and, with a drop
of spit in the wind, it was a blown berry,
what he wanted, if, ever-elusive.

She ran, taking with her the flown berry
from this lonely beast, leaving a bear of a burr,
reaped from the lawn of rye grass and violets,
sewn once by hand, by the delicate fingers
of his mother.

The Art of Shoveling

When you wake to the thick white quiet, don't despair.
When you know it will take hours to hours to remove
the two-foot, and still falling shroud, don't shy from it.

Before visualizing the entire driveway clear,
and you sailing out in your car, open the garage door.

From the dry floor, scoop up one shovelful and fling it
where you will not drive or walk.
Fling it in the air.

When, after a half hour, only a small square of blacktop
has emerged, and you have so much more,
start singing. *Yankee Doodle*, maybe.
You have earned one feather.

Before you start crying
you have no one you can call to help,
take out an audio book. *War and Peace*. Or *Catch 22*.
Something that will do the shoveling for you.

When the plow truck driver
tells you to get out of the way
and undoes your last hour's work,
don't waste your shaking fists.
Return the snow to the road
when the truck is gone.

When your back starts to feel the strain of the shovel,
mount your snowshoes. Be a piston. Float and sink.
Make troughs alongside your shovel area.
Somewhere to throw the snow.
A trap to catch it when it blows.

Night Swim

After a day's work at the home office,
after packing the car with camping gear,

after the long drive, slowed by traffic,
after pulling into the campground

and snagging the last spot on the pond,
after the hour it takes to park and set up the tent

in the darkening night, the dripping rain,
after finally eating what would constitute dinner:

four carrots with hummus, while seated,
dry in the driver's seat of my parked car.

After a day of not even stretching,
after gathering my swim gear, clothing, and towel,

headlamp affixed, I step down
the steep, root-strewn path that must lead to the pond.

At the water, in the almost pure dark,
the sky still drizzles.

Before stepping in, I strip,
and don my goggles, cap, and fins.

Before I set out, I make a mental note of my entry point,
and its surroundings:

> A big, secluded rock, a small cove,
> an opening in the trees. There is no moon.

My splashing strokes, the birds, and the constant drip.

By the time I am ready to stop swimming,
the sky is clear, the Big Dipper, revealed.

A Venus peers down at the lone nude,
swimming in the dark.

After I think I am nearing my entry point,
after trying one cove, and the next,

after every opening in the trees looks like the other,
after swimming in and out of each cove,

after approaching every big rock twice,
to find them blocked
by dead wood, (wrong),
grasses (wrong),
or other stones (wrong),

all the while, swimming, a repetition of coves.

After wishing for my glasses and my suit,
after considering a cry for help,

   Could I spend the night on a rock, or sleep in the shallows?

   Do the turtles sleep, and the fish, or do they nibble all night?

   Should I swim to a beach and walk out on the road,
   naked, without light?

I am Venus without her shell, only fins.
Would I purse my coy smile, if caught?

Green Dress

V-neck pinafore
V-chest
fastened with one stitch
to modest bubble breasts.
Breast band hugs ribs.
Green buttons spotted black, left,
gate the way to sleek hips
seeming even slicker
under spring leaf green drape.
Top, now perfect
sans the big fat square epaulettes.
Wings I finally shed last week
when I wore it with hope
to a date.

Bought in Paris
fifteen years past
having arrived there
via Romanian Airlines
from Bucharest,
where canned peas and cigarette smoke
held me Ceausescu's captive
in flight, even after leaving terra firma,
my border crossing to France,
my final release.

After some days,
I found the chic shops,
and, after trying so many:
What I can afford,
what is not tiny.
The goal
The stress
This dress
labeled Paris,
and after purchase, I notice,
made in Bucharest.

The Hard Side of Yellow

The tree is squat and fanned, a perfect umbrella.
That first summer, it held green fuzzy thimbles
until August.

In September, they hung like lanterns:
Tight ovals, not much bigger than golf balls.

Between worms, the grayish mold, and the squirrels,
how do you gauge when to pick?

Some years, there were hundreds. Others, ten.
Once, a raccoon tasted each hard green stone
and pitched it to the ground.

I have learned to pick early, just the hard side of yellow,
wash and leave them to ripen indoors.
Monitor, or lose the fruit to mold.

I'm from a long line of gatherers.
For a good harvest, I spend hours heating,
peeling, pitting, and sucking the warm meat off pits.

I freeze the stores
for when I will slave more hours over pies,
over warm peaches.

An Encounter at the Sink

When I walk into the kitchen to start the dishes,
the mold in my InSinkErator
says, *Carla, you're not a poet.*

I know, I say, a writer.
I've been a writer all my life.
But you, or any editor worth their spores
would say otherwise.

I took a hard look at your mechanism yesterday.
I felt around the blade, smooth.
Ran the motor. Heard the teeth
chewing and spitting, loud enough
to scare my fingers back into my pockets.
I couldn't find you, Mold.

Now, I am reminded of baking soda and bleach.
All the good I can do in this world to kill spores,
to get rid of you. You laugh, here to stay.
I will skirt your bleach. You are not a writer.
You're not even a mathematician.
You can count on that. Nice try.

One time, pumpkin seeds sprouted
from the disposal drain.
That was inspiring:
That something so fresh and vibrant,
so full of water, and green,
germinated from what seemed nothing.

Nothing? What am I, chopped liver?
A dark, dank, growing medium,
I'm alive. And things spring from me.

III. Décolletage

Counting

We will count to ten and time will collapse.
The snow starts its melt drop by drop,
from snow to ice. Rich mud becomes a puddle,
a trickle, a stream, a stream, a roaring river,
its stone walls gouged. I would call it a gorge,
but that sounds too gorgeous, one thing you called me
often. And now you're gone. How many days, months,
eons? I am still counting. I will count
to ten. To 100. I will hold our breath,
as mine is still yours, and suck
in all that water. The gorge
will collapse. The water,
dry up.

Décolletage

Undress me from turtleneck.
Roll your hand along my cords of throat.
Prick with silted fingertips.
Uncottoned kisses. Rose petal lips.

Weave me in. Can't be too tight.
Tight is not close enough.
Slide inside my silky sleeve.
Chest to chest, I wear you
braless. Keep me on.
You see, I am naked.
You nake me, neck down.

From the Beholder

Kiss me. Kiss me.
Slither and slide me.
Don't you know
what goes inside me?

Wake me. Rake me.
Press up close, baby.
It's you I crave, Mister
When you walk by me.

Not to Complain

1. Tea.

I grabbed the teabag from the canister marked, *Passion*,
a favorite, for the tea I made before I left to sing.
I drank it tonight last thing,
but didn't recognize the bergamot,
an old friend from long ago.
These days I don't take any caffeine,
so now, after the 20 mile bike ride, the choral concert,
the salon, and the escape from a rambling drunk,
I lie, not sleeping.

2. The Mechanic

Is it me I am mad at?
When my car returned from the mechanic,
the air comfort controller started to flash.
Intermittent was the word he used
when I called him back. Wiggling as many
empty words into my phrasing as possible,
I said I thought it had been his fault,
as he had been messing around in that area
to change a bulb. *It's not like it doesn't work,*
it just blinks a lot. He said he would call with a quote.
It's been months, now.
He's on my list to call once more.
Tell him, *Hey, it worked fine until you worked in there,*
this time with conviction.

3. The Marriage Bed

You devise divorce in sleep, and marriage in wake,
you, master of the twin beds.
You propose the game of musical bedrooms
will double our love.
I buy in, and lie awake, alone, in the other room,
in our king size.
I churn your missing warmth into missing you,
and wait for the elegant proof.

Lily Finds a Story About Jack on the Internet

Jack is sure he placed the small 19th century bas relief
frame he picked last week in the glove box,
after handing over a fifty.

The dealer had had no idea of the value.
With a potential buyer lined up,
Jack needs to find that treasure.

Jack looks in his car once more. The March night air
sears his skin. His torch runs dim.
He fumbles the lock, then he's in.

Hold it right there, he hears, from the right.
Jack remembers the gin he drank earlier.
He thinks, *This is my house, where I grew up. My car.
I don't need the Man in my face.*
Jack's face, sewn in a permanent frown. No one needs.

The policeman reads his rights. Jack wants his quiet night,
inside, to read more about beaten gold.

What is your name, the officer asks.
None of yours! Ah, there you are, my precious …
Jack turns to the frame.

It must have been the gin. Jack slams the door on the
officer's shin when he approaches the car.

The blotter reports a knock at the door. A woman opens,
Yes, I know him. My husband. "Arrested", it says. "Assault."

Lily tells her sister the story as she slices garlic. Husband.
Close call, her sister says. Another close call.

Knockoff

When you say
"Wouldn't it be better if you said..."
or "I saw your disappointment and felt cornered,
since I have a natural proclivity not to hurt,"
I hear you saying, *Knock it off.*

The week of the marathon bombs,
we were all emotional.
The dead and injured couldn't say *Knock it off,*
this was no joke.

Once, you knocked my socks off.
I might not have noticed,
but love came knocking — loud, insistent bursts.
Sometimes you encouraged me
to knock 'em dead, if my confidence waned.
Once, I knocked my ankle into a cinder block, when I fell
through a hole in your porch. Defending your house,
you knocked me down a notch, labeled me *accident-prone.*
You wanted to knock sense into me. Teach me
Knock it off. Your school of hard knocks.
Teacher, I have a question. Love doesn't make sense.

When a woman accidentally becomes pregnant,
she's *knocked up.* I swell up with feeling
when you tell me not to feel,
or how to feel,
or what not to say,
or, if I do say,
how to say it.

You wanted the cheap, knockoff feelings.
The *Yes, Sir, that's right. Whatever you want.*
Like the Walmart cashier
when you purchased a knockoff
scarf.

Self-Portrait in My Car

The new books stream in, eddying and piling up
around the passenger seat.
I take in the more popular, first,
and let the others slide.
Gish Jen. Her name, a stew.
I just returned one, almost due, unread.
And Patti Smith, *Just Kids*.
Oh that I would live on the edge
and make art with my very own vagabond sweetheart.

I hear the market is down again.
Maybe I won't retire yet.
But what do these fluctuations matter
if a shoe swimming at my feet,
catches under brake.
Congressman Barney Frank steps down.
He whines on the radio
of his missed fledgling academic career,
like the one I let go of all those years ago.
Who will hear my whine?

Sometimes I hug a canvas bag in my lap
as I drive so I don't forget
to take it with me when I disembark.
Will this be my air bag when I crash?
Will it be my singing that distracts? Rehearsing Brahms,
I try to make that high b-flat.
Traveling down the road in 3000 pounds,
I might just do that. Why sing with a chorus
when all the songs refer to Jesus in five languages.

Today the air is silky, swollen with damp,
and were I not responsible to my job
I would make use of the wetsuit in back,
or the bike that had been in the trunk
until last Sunday. I tell friends I still swim in the pond,
or that this November day or that
was my last. They wonder what will be the death of me.
But the more I go, the more I feel invincible.

What about that crackly wad of paper napkins
on the driver's floor?
A secret memento of a back seat rumble.
Unexpected groping
of two *just kids*, thought too old to fool around in cars:
Two who can't help but kiss.

The New Building

1.
The building, cantilevered atop a mountain,
overlooks the sea of traffic pooling at its feet.

Taillights, armies of workers, make their ways home.

You cry sleep from your eyes every morning
to avoid the slump of cars.

Agitation deepens
living in darkness without power.

Parking lots come out
of the building's ears.

2.
The rooms are not rooms.
Workstations, shrubs.
Burning bush, in greens and orange.
Sift through the flames to find your seat.

3.
The IT guy sees the photo of your boyfriend
before he was your boyfriend,
full up on your screen.
  The blue lake
  The sparkles of sunlight
  Shivers of waves
  The length of him
What the towel shields, no one smells.
A halo shimmers from his head.
A pyramid of light explodes.
He closes his eyes,
and dreams of your toes in his mouth.

You break the rules.
You wander the halls like a child
not learning not to complain.

Black Underwear

What I like about your black underwear
has little to do with the cloth
although it's cotton, it's soft.

Not so much the cut, but I see
your belly button up above the top,
the wide white elastic band of which

I like to pop with two fingers of one hand.
Maybe some, the color, for what it hides
and how it counters dark, however unnaturally,
your light.

What I like is what's inside, porcelain skin,
soft, grown hard, a color red, the color
of wine-stained linen, the color of cherry soup,

the weary color of my heart. Who
would sign a name to such togs, worn
like lilies on a salad, only to be tossed off?

Ginger Beer

Take a finger of ginger,
a thumb's worth
to the shredder.
Bring to a boil
a large pot of water,
then lower to simmer,
and add in the ginger.
Let it cook for a hour.
Add some honey.

Chill overnight,
and the ginger will settle.
Strain the ginger mixture into a bottle.
Honey for sweet, ginger for bite.
Sip it, share it, and delight.

The Prize

I remember our good times
more than your mean-heartedness.
The laughter, the cooking, the food.

I remember at the holiday party,
when you sat on the chair with the "lucky" ticket.

The glass bowl, the filters, the heater.
The money and time you spent.

How we named him Fernando,
our Betta fish. Some prize that was.

You had something to care for,
something more helpless than you,
and you thrived until we buried it.

The Flirt

Her saggy breasts bulge as she leans
tableward, like a ship on stormy sea. She
swings them up and down, shapes them to
his face as she talks. They pose a big question.
Beg it. *Will you come home with me? Will you love
me, sweet stranger?* She sits taller than the Girlfriend,
flustered green. Girlfriend wills her to put on a shirt,
but she waves victory with her bathing suit top,
pressing her flaccid pickles closer. Although she looks
only at him, her double barrels are aimed at both
of them. *Take this sweetheart. This is a test.
I have his number. Watch him
ask me for mine.*

IV. What Mother Didn't Know

Shrimp

1.
We lived in a slab house,
shingled and dark.
We were renting back then.
Mommy painted us.

My blue umbrella was satin,
just the right size for my hands.
It was not really for rain,
more a parasol.

Powder blue umbrella in hand,
I started to cross the street to Gina's.

2.
I remember lying in the driveway,
Mommy waiting impatiently
for the ambulance
that took forever.
Then Mommy holding my hand.

Then the wheelchair,
the hospital,
the teeth shaken out of me,
being carried everywhere
for a week before I regained my balance,
and the get well cards
from nursery school.

Later, the visit to a doctor,
supposed to check my hearing,
who put his hand so deep
I had to bury the memory.

3.
I never liked shrimp growing up.
I thought it was because Mommy only cooked it frozen,
and it smelled like a frozen toilet.

Later, Mom said I used to love shrimp,
and that the day I was hit by the car,
I threw it up on the driveway,
and after that, I wouldn't eat shrimp again.

It was a long time before I knew
shrimp didn't have to stink.
I never told Mom about the bad doctor.
By the time I remembered,
I knew what it smelled like,
and I didn't know what
I remembered.

Boyfriend

What did the mother think
when her daughter brought her new boyfriend
to the hospital, and he sat outside the whole time,
practicing his singing?
Oh, my daughter, what mistakes you are making?

Or was she close enough to the other side,
she could peer down from the future
and see what his simple acts of unkindness foretold?

As the poison dripped in her veins,
did she ponder how dry the air,
or the effort it took to stand?
Or did she take in the mere fact of *boyfriend*,
and stop there, smiling?

Did the daughter think, when her boyfriend went on
about how much he sacrificed
to travel all the way to New York,
that that was not much at all,
not even a small corner of her back,

which he was supposed to have,
those last days with her mother?
Or did she ignore these first signs,
take his hand in thanks,
and drink his medicine in great gulps?

Fall Leaves

I hate the trees.
Every fall the leaves,
whole piles swirl and spin
in the wind and land
in sheaves on the grass,
the driveway, the walk.

I slipped
on leaves yesterday.
Now, dead leaves stick
to the inside of my sweatshirt.

Mostly, I hate the pines.
The fine brown needles
don't prick, but lie flat,
a sticky thick carpet
woven brown,
ready to douse the yard
with acid.
I want to light the trees
on fire.

I never asked for so much.
The honey locust used to drop wheelbarrows
of pods yearly, until I chopped it down.

I do a little raking when I can.
Pine needles, where they pile up.
And I mow the leaves into the grass.

My mother always warned me to take care of the lawn.
If you let it go, it will cost thousands to replace.

School Picture

I keep the picture
in my family room,
for me, my family of one.
I pose on the shelf
as an angel,
the child I never had,
and look at the world
with hope.

It must have been taken
after the accident.
The photographer
coaxed my smile
without revealing
my missing teeth.

My top lip,
thin and long
and my lower lip,
rounded and curved.
Wisps of lightness arc over
my wide, smiling eyes.

My hands,
folded atop one another,
clasp under my chin.
Thick cherub wrists
are bent almost inhumanly
at right angles.
I am three, maybe four,
in nursery school.

I wear my favorite T-shirt:
Vertical ribs
with white and creamsicle sideways stripes.
My hair, a pageboy,
thick dark brown, and straight.
Bangs jag across my forehead.

I smile about something
I don't yet know.
I look up from long, curled lashes,
like I have an idea.

I hid in the bathroom, playing,
before my turn with the school photographer.
Was I telling Daniel I had seen my grandma
in her underwear?

The photo is black and white.
The glass, stippled
with spots of old dust
that cover my face.

Decisions

What eggs a mind that sees no future,
but four white walls,
and yet can find, somewhere in deep recesses
the triggers for a smile?

The sun shines through your yellow curtains.
Children laugh outside.
You rest on tear-stained pillows.
You don't know how to die.

You say, *Talk me out of this*, as if you have a choice.
Each moment, plump with loneliness
weights in along with graying vanity
against your wiry hair,

(*no point in dying anymore—who's to see?*)
and withered skin, and weakened bones.

No more games of bridge with other refugees,
walks among the banyan trees, or exhibits, at museums.
You've even had to let go of reading.

Jenny's children bring you smiles,
and I and others send our love.
I'd like to think not even pride could overcome
your fear of death, but could it?

Or would you follow, in Virginia's steps?
Memories turned in your fingers
from pebbles into stone?
Waiting for the inevitable,
from wading, to waiting to drown?

Indifference

When *I love you* yields her a blank stare.
she's at the point of not caring.
She has lost enthusiasm to return a knuckleball
of sarcasm, or to cry to him
how substandard she might feel for sticking it out
when his emotions are in the compost.
If a couple is supposed to care for one another,
he doesn't know.
He doesn't know from *supposed to.*
He knows *smile.*
He knows *shake hands.*
He knows the waggle penis.
He knows her day is Friday, and if Friday is taken,
then, next Friday, and not sooner.
He knows that when they watch movies,
he has his couch, and she, hers.
Same, with sleep and bedrooms.
She has learned all this. He teaches her well.
Once in awhile, a flicker of joy, a shared joke.
Once in awhile, they hold hands.
She tries *I love you.*
Sometimes he answers, *I love you, too.*
Sometimes, *That's nice.*

To Fire Island, By Counting

We were five 15 and 16 year olds. Two girls,
three guys. Mom never would have gone
for it, but she was gone to London on sabbatical,
and Dad was uninterested. *I'm going by bike*
to Fire Island with friends.
Mom would have demanded numbers:
How much they make. What their parents do for work.
Which religion. Phone numbers.
Before that day, 20 miles was my record,
an all-day affair. Now, forty-five miles from one end
of the island, and ten minutes to the last ferry
of the day (it was March, and ferries were spare),
two of the guys raced ahead and held it for us.
My young unmuscled legs protested,
while I withstood defeat. I was counting
on sleeping next to Marty that night,
and his two fingers my legs would swallow.

Pond Moment

Dive down the gradient
to the hot drinkable tea layer,
next, the cool green layer,
through to the cold blue slice of spring-fed chasm
where all the fishes must be.
That's where the fishermen are,
fishing from the dam, or in a rowboat.

The sun on your back would burn
without the cool water you kick up.
Your kick flows from long Cassiopeia legs.
Pull those spider arms, faster, faster.
Exhale slowly through your nose.
Take no air in until you turn your head,
catching the pines with a side glance,
and the next breath, three strokes later.
How beautiful you must look to anyone
who cares to see.

Tears in my Kitchen

Outside, my roof pillows,
soft waves of gray shingles.
Inside, above the kitchen shelves,
the tears line up like ducks
poised to drop, as if from a plane,
taking in the whole Zen sphere
of the counter and its crowded belongings
plop, plop, one by one,
to spread flat, and puddle.

The ceiling reveals old veins of glue,
the paper flaps like a torn blouse,
telling all.

From the Axiom of Choice to a Set of Measure Zero

You, with the rodeo belt, swinging figure eights,
hanging just below your waist.
Lasso me in. Lasso me in with Riemann,
Levis, and your square chin.

We converge, a slow descent, to a set of measure zero.
Those ballet shoes, those instruments,
those proofs you guide me through.

Oh a date on skates, on frozen lake, with toes to warm,
dinner to take. Hahn-Banach extensions
spaghetti over plate.

A kiss, unspoken, at end of lips, tongue, and tooth,
storied and moist. Realized, in mind,
our unwhispered wish, stirrings, unravelings,
uncontained, non-compact.

Pulled out of nowhere, from the same set,
New York/Texas:
Unsuspecting target for the *axiom of choice.*

Three Suits

A trio of Lycra suits hang singularly hooked, stretched.
Undue proportions, limp, sag-breasted,
flout slimming for large ladies, once floated, billowy.
Now, empty.

Autumn ghosts of Summer swims, dry now, cracked.
Each, black as funeral garb, worn, lace-empty,
thread-bare, Lycra spaghetti.

Each time I close the bathroom door,
the triptych begs,
                  Why three?
 Why does my mother hang three suits, equally worn?

These veils in waiting presage the answer:
one for each of us:
       Father
       Sister
       Me

Cheese Squash

And the farmer says, *the smoothest meat,*
or is that me?

And the meat is smooth, sweet,
not stringy, bitter.

And the skin is beige, like butternut,
not orange.

And the shape is ridged, cylindrical,
a squashed chef's hat.

And the seed is true, it does not mix.
Plant it.

And you get more pure sweet, not too,
and stringless.

And cull the drying stem from
prickly vine.

And draw the knife, a circle around the stem,
tug the top.

And scoop the flat moist seeds and
spare, ropey pulp.

And replace the lid before baking the beast,
an hour, 400 degrees.

And the roasted brown skin collapses
into itself.

And the clear, golden juice spills, fills the pan,
sweet, fresh, nourishing milk.

And dig up the baked squash, contain it,
squeezing the remaining juice.

And put it up to freeze, until ready
to make pies.

And thaw to bake, expunging more juice
to drink.

And roll the dough flat on marble,
to keep it cool.

And fill the pans with rolled dough,
and beat filling.

And bake in a hot oven,
short to brown,

And lower the temperature,
until done.

And knife-test the browned custard,
until it holds a cut.

And remove, let cool,
and slice.

And taste the pie wedge,
and *Ooh.*

And tell anyone who will listen,
of the meat of the story, of the pure strain.

Mother, He Spins Me Around

My friends ask if I'm still seeing him.
He's nice, I affirm, embarrassed.
He's smart. He's generous. I like him.
You would have liked him.

The other day I said I thought he was *on the spectrum.*
Thoughtless, I know. But that's what I was thinking.
I wanted to elaborate, start a conversation,
but these days we avoid the touchy spots.

He still kisses me. Says, "Sometimes
it's your turn. Sometimes, mine."

I think I am getting somewhere, and maybe I am.
Now he accepts my invitations to dance.

Tonight we dance under the skies.
He tells me a story about his brother.
How he doesn't miss him, either.

Mother, One More Thing

A Wellfleet house with sloped ceilings and white walls,
pink light through the trees early morning.
Three large casements on two walls and a skylight.
The ceiling follows the slope of the roof.
The casement on the north wall, raised.
Outside, inside our bedroom.

Copies of famous paintings, sprinkled throughout
in subdued reds, browns, blacks, and whites.
The furnishings, simple, from the fifties,
with minor updates each decade.

Mother, you don't know this, you haven't been there.
One corner we never explored. The paintings belong
to the owners. In good taste, but not yours.

Best of all, the pond. It has your name.
I slip in every morning for a swim.
Right after you come to me in dream. After I stretch.
After the subjugation resembling love.

CPSIA information can be obtained at www.ICGtesting.com
Printed in the USA
BVOW08s1249110214

344576BV00003B/6/P